12-8-04

(R) only copy

M

CHILDREN'S DEPARTMENT

THE BRUMBACK LIBRARY

OF VAN WERT COUNTY

VAN WERT, OHIO

LEARN THE VALUE OF

Fairness

◆

by ELIZABETH COTE

Illustrated by Dorey E. Evans

◆

ROURKE ENTERPRISES, INC.
VERO BEACH, FL 32964

Library of Congress Cataloging-in-Publication Data

Cote, Elizabeth, 1957–
    Learn the value of fairness/by Elizabeth Cote;
illustrated by Dorey Evans.

    1. Fairness—Juvenile literature.   I. Evans, Dorey.
II. Title.   III. Title: Fairness.
BJ1533.F2C68   1989   179' .9—dc19   89-23978
ISBN 0-86592-445-7   *LCCN 88-23978*

Fairness

Do you know what **fairness** is?

Fairness is taking turns twirling the rope as well as jumping rope.

Fairness is cleaning up together after your snack.

Mom is being **fair** when she gives my sister and
me two cookies each.

Fairness is giving part of your allowance to
your brother because he helped you do the dishes.

Letting your brother or sister sit in the new chair because you sat in it the night before is being **fair.**

Fairness is cutting a cake into pieces that are all the same size.

Fairness is taking your little brother to the library
story hour because you promised him you would.

Fairness is letting your friend pick the movie
you go to see since you picked the last one.

When your teacher chooses a line leader from names put into a hat, that's being **fair.**

Making a time chart so that everyone
gets a chance to use the computer at school,
that's being **fair.**

Fairness is helping your friend with her paper
route because she helped you fix your bike.

Being **fair** is taking turns choosing which television show to watch.

Fairness is doing your share of the chores.

Fairness is taking care of your little brother
so that Mother can read a book.

Sharing the responsibilities of caring for a pet as well as having fun with it is being **fair.**

Fairness is waiting your turn in line instead
of cutting ahead.

Fairness is letting everyone play in the game, even if some may not be as good at it as others.

930066

Fairness is treating others the way you want them to treat you.

Fairness

The recess bell rang and everyone filed out to the playground.

Brian grabbed the kickball on his way out and yelled, "Come on! Let's play! I'll be the pitcher!"

"You're always the pitcher, Brian. I'd like to try it," protested Danny.

"I got here first, so I get to be the pitcher."

"You should let someone else pitch," said Levon. "Why don't you play in the field today?"

"I'd like a turn at pitching, too," said Lillian. So did Debbie, Eli and Cam.

"Well, we can't all pitch," said Levon. "Since there are five who want to be pitchers, we can have one for each day of the week. Danny can pitch today."

Which children knew about being **fair?**
How do you try to find **fair** solutions to problems that come up?

Fairness

Karen, Jenny and Ryan decided they wanted to make some money. They were going to rake Mr. Johnson's lawn on Saturday morning. They had planned to meet there at 9:00. Karen arrived right on time, got a rake from the garage and started working.

Jenny and Ryan came to the yard an hour later.

"Did you oversleep?" asked Karen.

"No," said Ryan. "A good cartoon came on TV, so we stayed to watch it."

By noon, they were done raking the yard.

Mr. Johnson came out to pay them. "Looks great. You kids did a good job." He handed them $15.00 dollars.

"Wow, we each get five dollars!" said Ryan.

"No. Karen should get more. She was here longer than us," said Jenny. "She should get $6.00 and we should each get $4.50."

Which child was being **fair?**
What would you have done if you were Ryan? Jenny? Karen?